THE EYE OF THE NEEDLE

Autosculpture, *Hagop Sandaldjian, c. 1984*

CONTRIBUTIONS FROM THE MUSEUM OF JURASSIC TECHNOLOGY

THE EYE OF THE NEEDLE

The Unique World of Microminiatures of Hagop Sandaldjian

Essay by Ralph Rugoff

PUBLISHED BY THE TRUSTEES

*funded in part by the City of Los Angeles Cultural Affairs Department
and the members of the Museum with the kind assistance of ARTS, Inc.*

*This book is dedicated to
the memory of Hagop Sandaldjian.*

WHENEVER we encounter some truly novel phenomenon, one that reinvents the margins of our world, an old hankering is awakened. At such moments we are like explorers of an unknown dimension: everything appears fresh to our eyes, each idea seems unprecedented, virgin, strange. In the face of this newly made universe, we may be tempted to exclaim "It cannot be!" yet our protests soon lie buried under an avalanche of wonder, and a desire to escape the narrow limits of our existence takes hold once again.

An experience of this nature may enter your life, penetrating as silently and inexorably as a stone sinking in still waters, when you encounter the microminiature sculpture of Hagop Sandaldjian. On first entering an exhibition of his work, however, one observes little of interest: there is no art immediately visible, only a prosaic collection of transparent acrylic canopies, each housing a small viewing apparatus of approximately 25-power magnification. Within each casing one can discern little more than a simple sewing needle, usually suspended at a perpendicular angle from a slender brass post; near the tip or within the eye of each needle, the unassisted observer can just make out a tiny speck of what appears to be a routine species of grit.

Only in the private view afforded by each eyepiece are the demure splendors of this art revealed. What had seemed no more than a filament of dust proves to be a carved and painted sculpture of Mickey Mouse (plate 12), shown balancing on a single leg atop the point of a needle; his outstretched arms, thinner than a bissected strand of hair, culminate in white gloves so fine as to be barely perceptible. Framed within the eye of another needle a stern-faced Napoleon (plate 1), dressed for battle and heroically posed on a craggy pedestal, beckons with an imposing presence, although his entire frame is no larger than the period that ends this sentence.

It was Napoleon who declared "Imagination rules the world," yet Sandaldjian's tiny figures seem to rule a world of unimaginable dimensions. When we first behold such astounding and disorienting sights, disbelief is not an uncommon response. Our skepticism is piqued by our lack of direct visual access, and we regard the mediating microscope with suspicion, as though its minute optical theater might be the scene of possible manipulation and chicanery. One keeps hoping to see "how it's done," to discover the secret behind this impossible illusion, because it is easier to believe in trickery than to accept the truth of Sandaldjian's work, a truth that seems to unsettle the line between reality and dream.

Sandaldjian's microminiatures, reproduced and enlarged on these pages for the reader's pleasure and contemplation, were fashioned from slivers of human hair and motes of dust and glue. Peering through a 120-power microscope,

Sandaldjian carved and painted sculptures measurable in microns and millimeters; his *Pope John Paul II* (plate 28) holds a cross crafted from a hair divided into sixths, making its width slightly less than the diameter of two red blood cells. His portrait of Little Red Riding Hood (plate 26), whose diminutive has never been so well deserved, features a mere speck of a girl lost amid a towering grove of trees in a needle's eye; only after one's eyes have grown accustomed to the microscopic detail is it possible to see that she carries a tiny basket in her hands.

Sculpture on this scale seems utterly miraculous, yet it simultaneously evinces an aura of consummate modesty; Sandaldjian's entire oeuvre would easily rest in an infant's hand. In an age when artists tend towards grandiose spectacles, his work is a gift that can be given to just one person at a time, drawing us individually into an enchanted and bewildering space. Looking down on Napoleon's rocky pedestal, which drops away on each side like a sheer cliff, viewers may come to know a strange new vertigo.

If the size of Sandaldjian's work is astonishing, equally so is the expressive range he achieves on this scale. Exquisitely carved, his sculpture employs a small arsenal of spatial and painterly effects. Subjects strike expressive, fully articulated poses that economically convey a sense of their psychological character: standing stiffly in his papal regalia, John Paul II radiates ceremonial calm and dignity. In another sculpture, Goofy (plate 8), depicted with precariously swaying limbs and torso, provides a study in freewheeling abandon.

Sandaldjian was also a sensitive colorist, capable of balancing over a dozen brilliant hues in a single piece and setting them against a monochrome background. Works such as *Snow White and the Seven Dwarfs* (plate 7), a memorable group portrait posed along a needle's edge, demonstrate his command of nuance as well, evident in flawlessly realized details like Doc's spectacles and Sleepy's whimsically angled cap. These technical achievements amount to far more than a display of craftsmanship; they lie at the heart of Sandaldjian's ability to transform stock subjects into compelling sculpture.

For Sandaldjian, the advantage of using familiar icons was not simply that they are readily recognizable at any size, but that we bring to them a history of imaginative investment. By showing us only the gestalt of a subject, stunning us with an evocative handful of details rather than a hyperrealistic rendering, his microscopic renderings lead us to draw upon that history. The artist's use of a viewing microscope of only 25 power, a level of magnification at which his work still appears too small to be closely scrutinized, reinforces this, as we are left to complete the details in our imagination.

Utterly transformed by their impossible scale, Sandaldjian's figures appear at once banal and elusive, meticulously crafted and dreamily insubstantial. Each nearly weightless sculpture seems to hover between its slim hold on the material plane and the lucid and immeasurable reality of a mental image. The work's microscopic size, meanwhile, conjures the field of science rather than art. Miniaturization, one of the defining motifs of modern life, is commonly associated with the development of military and space technologies, computers and communication media, and more recently, with nanotechnologists who create motors micromachined for shafts the size of a human hair.[1] Haunted by these allusions, Sandaldjian's sculpture seems to straddle the line between science, craft, art, and novelty. In the end, it befuddles our ability to make such distinctions, and in so doing opens a space for wonder.

Before he passed away in 1990, Sandaldjian was one of only four or five living practitioners of microminiature, a Slavic specialty that is understandably rare because it demands unthinkable physical precision. "Working through the microscope requires not only control of the hand and of one's breathing, but of the entire nervous system," Sandaldjian remarked. "The slightest misdirected movement can destroy the very form being shaped in a fraction of a second."[2] Since even a pulse in his fingers could cause an accident, Sandaldjian ultimately learned to apply his decisive strokes only between heartbeats.

Remarkably, he was not actually a sculptor by profession, but a musician, teacher, and theorist. By all accounts a passionate man, he entwined his warm humor and generosity around an abiding faith in our power to realize the most far-flung dreams. And in his path to mastering this extraordinary and obsessive art—the accomplishment of a lifetime in itself—he drew on all facets of his rich character and background.

≈≈

The second of three children, Hagop Sandaldjian was born in Alexandria, Egypt, in 1931. As a child he showed little

Hagop Sandaldjian in 1931 at six months of age.

Hagop at six years of age, accompanying his sister, Sona, on his first violin.

interest in music, but he excelled in mathematics and had a remarkable capacity for throwing himself wholeheartedly into any activity he pursued. When enlisted by his father, a businessman who also acted in the Armenian theater, to play the role of a poor, dying waif in a local production, the ten-year-old Hagop identified so ardently with his part that when his character expired on stage at the end of the first performance, Hagop fainted and had to be rushed to a doctor.

As a teenager, Sandaldjian found an outlet for his emotional intensity in the fervor of postwar Armenian nationalism. Caught up in a whirlwind of patriotic feeling, he announced to his family that he had no choice but to obey his heart and move to Armenia. His parents, perhaps impressed by the force of his conviction, agreed to accompany him. In 1948 the entire family left Cairo, where they had been living, and resettled in Yerevan, the capital of what was then Soviet Armenia.

Two years earlier, Sandaldjian had begun playing the violin, discovering what was to be a lifelong love of music. His father, upset that his son seemed bent on pursuing an

Eight years of age.

impractical career, went so far as to smash Hagop's first violin, but this attempt at dissuasion was to no avail. Against his parents' wishes, Hagop later enrolled in Yerevan's Romanos Melikian Music College. Headstrong as ever, he had set his sights on becoming a virtuoso, despite his inauspiciously late start.

He compensated for his lack of experience with endless hours of practice. After completing his studies in Yerevan, he immediately enrolled in the Ippolitov Ivan Music College in Moscow, from which he gradu-

Sixteen years of age, as the family prepared to move to Armenia.

ated in 1955. Eight years later he emerged from Moscow's celebrated Komitas State Conservatory with a master's degree in the performing arts.

Settling in Yerevan with his wife, Verena, a choir conductor and teacher whom he had met while studying at the Melikian Music College, Sandaldjian threw himself into the capital's lively music scene. Along with teaching at two music colleges and the state conservatory, Sandaldjian also became a highly regarded soloist with the national orchestra. Composers began to write pieces specifically for him, and his performances on Armenian National Radio made him a well-known figure in the city's cultural life. By the standards of the day, he was materially well rewarded; he lived with his wife and their two young children, Siranush and Levon, in a roomy four-bedroom apartment on Bagramian Street, a prosperous boulevard near the city's center.

Cairo Mekhitarist College graduating class, 1946.

Amid the pressing engagements of a busy career, San-daldjian somehow found time to pursue a wide range of other interests. He became a skilled practitioner of yoga. He kept bees. He nurtured a great love of village life and would often spend a day in the countryside, fishing or playing Gypsy music with friends, returning home to quickly don his formal attire and rush off to another performance.

In the early 1970s one of his viola students at the conservatory introduced him to yet another avocation. The student, Edward Kazarian, was several years older than Sandaldjian and was already renowned as a microminiaturist who had exhibited his work internationally. A deep friendship soon blossomed between these two artists, and they arrived at a unique agreement by which each became the other's student: Sandaldjian would impart his knowledge of music, and Kazarian would share the secrets of his minuscule craft.

Fate could not have brought Kazarian a better pupil. While many would have been daunted by the dexterity and concentration demanded by microminiature art, Sandaldjian was peculiarly suited to the task; it presented him in fact with an opportunity to test further the theory of ergonomics he had been developing since the early 1960s.

As a late starter on the violin, Sandaldjian found that his hands tired and ached after hours of practice. Impressed with virtuosos who could play difficult pieces seemingly without strain and for long stretches of time, he methodically sought out a means to duplicate their success, and he eventually turned to ergonomics, the study of efficient interaction between people and the tools they use. Though ergonomics was principally associated with research in industry and sport, Sandaldjian became convinced that such an applied science might also enable musicians to improve their muscle control.

According to general ergonomic theory, every time we use a tool we pit an inner force—the contraction of muscles—against an outer force: terrestrial gravitation. Fluent, proficient performance results from the harmonious resolution of these opposing forces. To be successful as a violinist, Sandaldjian concluded, one needed to maintain "a good relationship with gravity." This could only be achieved by abandoning the standard teaching approaches, which tended to focus on "correct" finger positions, for a method that accommodated the individual anatomy of each student.[3]

Hagop stung by one of his bees, Yerevan, 1963.

*Hagop Sandaldjian playing violin with
the Yerevan Theater Orchestra, early 1950s.*

In drawing on ergonomics as a teacher, Sandaldjian came to believe that it could help even average students become accomplished musicians. "Our pedagogical observations and scientific experiments . . . have demonstrated that the rational use of gravitational force ensures the continuous beauty of sound as well as saves the time and energy of the performer," he declared in one of his many papers on the subject.[4] Child prodigies owed their early achievements, he explained, to the fact that they intuitively followed the rational rules of musical performance outlined by ergonomics.

In 1973 Sandaldjian presented his thesis—that paper we know in English as "The Perfected Position of Viola and Its Significance for Musical Performance"—before the highest committee of the Moscow Conservatory. It was approved by a rare unanimous vote, and Sandaldjian's teaching methods were eventually introduced into the official curriculum. As if responding to the needs of socialist science, they seemed to herald a future where every worker could also be a part-time virtuoso.

Sandaldjian published numerous articles on ergonomics, but perhaps his crowning achievement in this field was his performance at a 1977 Moscow conference of viola players. Playing a viola pomposa, a twenty-inch-long, five-stringed instrument that had been neglected for almost two hundred years due to its unwieldy size, Sandaldjian performed several works by Johann Sebastian Bach. His masterful playing stunned the audience and led to a mild revival of interest in an instrument long considered to be impossible to master.

⇜⇝

While Kazarian was eagerly pursuing his musical studies, Sandaldjian had been gradually acquiring the skills of the

*Edward Kazarian and Hagop Sandaldjian
with viola pomposa, Yerevan, 1973.*

Playing the viola pomposa, 1973.

microminiaturist. Having obtained an adequate microscope, he began to experiment with appropriate sculptural materials, testing the hair of different family members for texture, tone, and tensile strength. His first completed work, *Autosculpture* (plate 24), appropriately used one of his own black hairs for a three-dimensional carving of the top of his balding head—the very image he had presented to the world during the weeks he spent hunched over his laborious creation. With this droll flourish, Sandaldjian seemed to declare that no matter how painstaking and obsessive his new endeavor might be, he would keep his humor in play.

As a tribute to his friendship with Sandaldjian, for whom he felt tremendous affection as both his teacher and student, Kazarian painted their joint portrait on a grain of rice. Yet ultimately, despite his mentor's constant encouragement, Sandaldjian was too busy as a performer and teacher to pursue microminiature sculpture as much more than a hobby. It was not until he arrived in the United States that circumstances conspired to leave him the time needed to hone his skills and master this most challenging medium.

Among his many talents, Hagop Sandaldjian believed he had prophetic abilities; in particular, he felt he could receive forebodings of impending disaster. During the late 1970s he came to understand that grave upheavals would soon threaten Armenia, and in 1980 he gathered his family and emigrated to Los Angeles. As a condition of his departure, customs officials forced Sandaldjian to leave behind his entire collection of eighteen microminiatures, declaring it a national treasure that could not leave the country. For Sandaldjian this was no small sacrifice, but his uncanny premonition of Armenia's future upheavals compelled him to put this personal loss aside.

In Los Angeles Sandaldjian found himself in a strange milieu where the achievements of his distinguished career were largely unknown. Settling in Hollywood, he was unable to find significant employment as either a violinist or a music teacher. Disheartened by the lack of concrete

Hagop with other members of the conservatory faculty, Yerevan, 1978.

prospects, he turned his attention to the less tangible world of microminiature, finding in its cozy dimensions a welcome sanctuary from the frustrations of his new life. Far from fleeing practical concerns, however, Sandaldjian initially envisioned his tiny art as the means to a viable livelihood; in a country where everything was for sale, he felt certain he could earn a decent income by selling microscopic sculpture.

While Verena supported the family by taking on sewing jobs at home, often working both day and night, Sandaldjian applied himself with his usual confidence and inexhaustible energy. He had of course no difficulty procuring his preferred sculptural materials—hair and dust—but now that he was undertaking microminiature work in earnest, he needed a proper tool kit. As no art supply store in the world carries such delicate items, Sandaldjian fashioned his own specialized instruments from scratch, grinding diamond dust and ruby powder and joining motes of these crushed gems to the points of filed-down needles. For his paintbrushes he sharpened individual strands of hair.

An artist who works on so diminutive a scale must not only possess adequate tools; he must also maintain a tender sensibility, a quiet and dexterous hand, and a fastidious spirit. The noted seventeenth-century English miniaturist Edward Norgate advised that "the practicer of limning be preizly pure and klenly in all his doings. . . . At the least let your aparrel be silke, such as sheadeth lest dust or haires, weare nothing straight, and take heed of the dandrawe of the head sheading from the hairs, and of speaking ouer your worke for the least sparkling of spettel will never be hoplen if it light on the face or any part of the naked."[5]

*Hagop and Verena Sandaldjian at an
Armenian cultural reception, Los Angeles, 1986.*

Sandaldjian did not wear silk when he sculpted, but he did take other precautions: he worked alone in a quiet room, and usually only late in the night when static-bearing dust particles had settled and the rumbling of passing cars and trucks had died down. To calm his mind he would occasionally don a pair of headphones and listen to the music of Bach.

The first sculpture he completed in Hollywood, a microscopic cluster of red grapes, was dedicated to the labor of his wife, who after two years of sewing had recently found new employment as a teacher. Entitled *Prosperity* (plate 15), it incorporates the last needle Verena used on her sewing machine: suspended within the needle's eye Sandaldjian's impeccable grapes shimmer with gold highlights and subtly varied hues. To render form so exquisitely seems, on some level, nothing less than an act of love.

Sandaldjian regarded each finished sculpture with a parent's protective gaze. He would complete a piece only to acknowledge that it was too precious to part with. In practical terms, this attitude ensured that his commercial aspirations were never realized; though he eventually obtained a business license, he never sold a single microminiature sculpture.

Born of obsessive devotion, an individual figure could take as many as fourteen months to finish. Each sculpted micron represented not only endless hours of toil, but exacting travail fraught with peril, as his work could so easily be destroyed or lost. An unexpected sneeze or misdirected breath could blow away a microminiature with hurricane force, while a casual movement could sabotage the work of months. In the course of his labors Sandaldjian lost numerous pieces, including several Napoleons and a supremely graceful ballerina he refused to reattempt. Early on in his career he would spend hours hunting for these missing children, carefully combing every inch of desk and floor space in his study, but eventually he realized that such searching was futile. Once a piece was lost, it was lost for good.

Painting his microminiatures posed yet another complex challenge. "Paint is a dictator," Sandaldjian frequently observed. "A misplaced drop can swallow and destroy the perspective of the whole work." He tirelessly experimented with diverse pigments and thinners to obtain a workable consistency. Because the tiny specks of paint he used would dry in seconds on the tips of his single-hair brushes, he had to work with speed as well as precision, while making the smallest imaginable movements. To those who watched him paint, it often seemed as if his hands never even moved.

Such sureness of touch requires exceptional powers of composure. Sandaldjian's equilibrium seems all the more remarkable given his volatile personality. He was a man of tremendous emotion and drama who preferred to be constantly in motion. "He was always jumping up and down with excitement," his daughter, Siranush, recalls, and in the stormy symphonies of Beethoven, which he revered, he found a sympathetic reflection of his own overflowing vitality. Yet Sandaldjian clearly had the ability—perhaps developed from his ergonomic and yogic exercises—to concentrate his passionate energy into a laserlike point of calm.

After laboring out of the public view for a number of years, Sandaldjian mounted his first exhibition in March 1986 at the Los Angeles Design Center Art Gallery, an event sponsored by the Armenian Allied Arts Association. In its range of motifs, the show embraced an international perspective: eye-of-a-needle portraits of Napoleon and a Spanish dancer (plate 4) were displayed alongside a grain of rice bearing the Arabic inscription: "There is no God but Allah, and Mohammed is his Prophet"; another grain of rice incorporated verses of Charents' poetry beneath a drawing of Ararat's twin peaks, legendary home of Noah's ark (plate 23). The culture of Sandaldjian's adopted home, meanwhile, was represented by microminiature sculptures of Donald Duck (plates 10 and 11) and several other Disney characters (plates 7–9 and 12).

Distinctly eclectic, even ecumenical, this sundry assortment of motifs reflected the artist's desire that his work be accessible to a wide audience. Sandaldjian seems to have

At Disneyland with Verena and Siranush, 1982.

envisioned microscopic space as a universal forum and accordingly, microminiature sculpture as a medium suited to monumental subjects. During his Los Angeles years, he focused his art almost exclusively on larger-than-life figures from history, myth, and popular culture, while creating only one piece, *Broken Dreams* (plate 3), that referred to his personal history. Measuring one thirty-secondth of an inch in length, it features a golden violin with a broken neck, laid out across a tiny black pedestal. Recalling the incident from his youth when his disapproving father had smashed his violin, it also hints at the more recent trauma of his shattered hopes for a musical career in the United States.

Brilliant in use of color and detail, the work in Sandaldjian's debut exhibition demonstrated that he had surpassed even his mentor Kazarian. Around this same time Sandaldjian's improving musical fortunes provided another source of satisfaction. In 1986 he gained an appointment as an associate professor of music at California State College, Los Angeles, and his Komitas Music School, which he ran with his wife and daughter from their home, had become a successful base for spreading the gospel of ergonomics.

Sandaldjian plunged into his teaching activities with an ardor and generosity that inspired profound devotion in many of his students. "May all your dreams come true," he would tell them, speaking with irresistible conviction and warmth. He seemed to possess an almost magical skill in guiding a novice's unsteady progress with cogent instructions and descriptions. "He had a great hue of words that immediately made the light click on in the student's mind," recalled one former pupil. Beyond his pedagogical skills, Sandaldjian touched his students with a quality of contact that seemed to illuminate their lives. "He had the power to turn everything dark into something good," explained the father of another longtime pupil. "His home was like a church for us, and he was the priest."

Despite the demands of his revived professional career, Sandaldjian avidly pursued his microminiature work, encouraged by the warm public response to his 1986 show, which received reviews not only in Los Angeles' local Armenian newspapers, but on the front page of the *Wall Street Journal* and the *New York Times*. Yet even though individual viewers were frequently awed by his sculpture, there seemed to be something about microminiature that prevented many people from considering it seriously—they regarded it as a mere novelty or divertisement, hardly the stuff of great art. Certainly it shared none of the prestige and dignity associated with classical music, yet Sandaldjian became increasingly dedicated to his tiny art and sought out new opportunities to exhibit it.

In 1987 his efforts were recognized with a prize from the National Small Works Competition, juried that year by a curator from New York's Guggenheim Museum of Art. The award was given for *Wild Animals* (plate 19), a sprightly procession of twelve jungle creatures painted on a hair. The following year, Sandaldjian exhibited eight works at the Metropolitan Museum in Fresno, California. And then in December of 1990, a show of nearly two dozen microminiatures opened at The Museum of Jurassic Technology in Los Angeles. Planned with the artist's active cooperation, the exhibition would, alas, serve as a memorial tribute, as Sandaldjian unexpectedly passed away a month before it opened.

Hagop Sandaldjian left behind a total of thirty-three microminiatures. In the family's Southern California home, where his wife has preserved his workshop much as it once was, his final and unfinished work is displayed. It is a reverent portrait of Mekhitar of Sebaste, the bearded eighteenth-century founder of the Mekhitarist Congregation, whose school Sandaldjian had attended in Cairo. Barely perceptible even when viewed through a microscope, it is the tiniest portrait Sandaldjian ever attempted. Today it stands as a reminder of an artist who, even in his last days, never ceased exploring the frontiers of the possible.

In his study the artist's microscopes and handmade tools remain on his desk, issuing a silent challenge to each visitor. "It has been done before me, and if I can do it, others can too," Sandaldjian modestly maintained. Although he was unassuming about his achievements, he stressed that those

Hagop Sandaldjian at work.

who were interested in joining him in this rare and singular field must be willing to cultivate "the talents of an artist, a craftsman, and above all the patience of a saint."

Few in the world have such patience. Of the handful inspired to try mastering this art, only a small percentage have succeeded. Several would-be microminiaturists have gone blind in the process, and estimates by knowledgeable authorities, such as Nikolai Syadristy of Kiev, suggest that today there may be only four or five living practitioners, all of them residing within the boundaries of the former Soviet Union.[6]

Though the history of microminiature art remains shrouded in obscurity, we can assume that microminiature is among the youngest of arts, since its development is necessarily linked to that of the microscope. This optical instrument, so indispensable to modern science, first appeared during the great period of the *wunderkammer;* by 1673 the Dutch naturalist Antonie van Leeuwenhoek had already developed lenses of sufficient power to observe bacteria a mere three microns in diameter. Slightly less important to our tiny field, but hardly negligible, was the invention of the lathe, which allowed microsculptors to work with a degree of precision previously unobtainable.

Technology, of course, was not the only factor contributing to the rise of microminiature. The age's spirit of discovery, evident in both its scientific and geographical exploration, no doubt prepared practitioners for the possibility of venturing into unseen realms. Indeed, more than one authority has suggested that the genesis of microminiature sculpture may have been influenced, at least in part, by Gottfried Wilhelm Leibniz's theory of *petites perceptions.* A seventeenth-century German philosopher and mathematician, Leibniz held we may entertain perceptions so delicate and minute that our awareness of them skirts the field of consciousness yet nevertheless registers some ineffable mental effect.[7]

In the fifteenth and sixteenth centuries, however, miniature carved portraits and bas-reliefs had already become extremely popular in Europe and England, establishing a taste for finely detailed renderings and perhaps helping to pave the way for the first examples of that extremely small work known by the French as *la sculpture microscopique.* The nineteenth-century English authority J. L. Propert cites two noteworthy examples in his *History of Miniature Art.* After discussing Prosperzia de Rossi, a renowned gem engraver from Bologna who carved a passion scene including Christ, the Apostles, the fourteen stations of the cross, the executioners, and a crowd of onlookers on a single peach stone, Propert goes on to describe the celebrated knife of Leo Pronner of Nuremberg, created for an Archduke of Austria in 1606:

> The length of the handle was ten centimetres (four inches), and was divided into thirteen drawers. In these drawers were stowed away the psalms, written on parchment in twenty-one languages, 1500 different tools, 100 pieces of gold, a chain fifteen centimetres long, composed of 100 rings, a cherry-stone carved with armorial bearings, twenty-four tin plates, twelve knives with steel blades and wooden handles, and forks to match, twelve wooden spoons, and a human hair divided in its thickness into ten parts.[8]

It is not known whether either of the above-mentioned artists made use of early models of the microscope.

Curiously, allusions to things of microminiature dimension appear in myths, folktales, and scripture long before work of this size could be physically realized. In the Middle Ages theologians debated the precise number of angels that could dance on the head of a pin, believing the angels' infinitesimal size to be a sign of the Creator's immeasurable powers. Mortal creatures of microscopic proportion appear in folktales such as *Tom Thumb* and its various adaptations. Among the collected tales of Charles Perrault, a popular seventeenth-century fabulist, we find a character named Petit Poucet, who is so small that during one adventure he "splits a grain of dust with his head, and passes through it with his entire body."[9]

Similar examples abound in English literature. In *Gulliver's Travels*, Jonathan Swift's traveling hero observes a

Lilliputian girl sewing with a needle too small to be seen, and Lewis Carroll's famous Alice becomes so tiny that she nearly drowns in one of her giant tears. In some cases, there is evidence that comparable stories exerted a direct influence on microminiaturists: Nikolai Syadristy, the self-taught master of Kiev, began his first microscopic work in 1959 after reading a Russian folktale about an ambitious courtier who sought to impress the Czar by presenting him with a shod flea. (Syadristy's sculpture, a preserved flea outfitted with shoes made from flecks of gold, is housed on the grounds of the Pecherskaya Lavra, an eleventh-century Russian Orthodox monastery in Kiev, where it is displayed at a magnification of 64 power.)[10]

Unrestricted by the physical responsibilities of dimension, the literary imagination continues to conjure vistas of infinite smallness. The allure of this conceit engages the popular imagination in contemporary science-fiction tales and in comic-book characters such as Atom Ant, the first microscopic superhero, and it has been a staple of Hollywood films as well, including *Fantastic Voyage* (1966), *Inner Space* (1987), and *Honey I Shrunk the Kids* (1989), all of which depict modern scientific methods for drastically reducing the volume and mass of human beings.

When such a fantastical motif endures through the ages, weathering the changing whims of human fancy and thriving in diverse cultural climates, we must wonder at the secret of its undying, and seemingly universal, appeal. What depths of our soul, what invisible yearnings and appetites, are so enchanted by the mere thought of microminiature dimension? And what is the particular nature of the spell it casts?

If we proceed with caution, remembering the delicate nature of the object of our study, some glimmering may be given us to illuminate these mysteries. Because this minuscule art seems to exist in a world apart, defying all standards of measure, we must approach it indirectly or it will elude us, since without benefit of comparison we cannot properly gauge its true character. By first considering the case of simple miniatures, the specific qualities of the microminiature, which are of an entirely different nature, may gradually become clearer.

⁊⃑⸾⃑

Encompassing painting, sculpture, and writing, the tradition of the "tiny arts" has a long and impressive history, having flourished at one time or another in ancient Sumer, Greece, Egypt, China, Byzantium, Persia, India, Africa, and throughout Europe. In antiquity, little books in particular were cultivated. According to Pliny, Cicero reported seeing a volume of the *Iliad* no larger than a nutshell, and in another ancient account, Aelian tells of an artist who enclosed a verse couplet, written in letters of gold, inside the rind of a grain of corn. In his *Curiosities of Literature,* nineteenth-century author Isaac D'Israeli cites these examples and observes that "Antiquity and modern times record many such penmen, whose glory consisted in writing in so small a hand that the writing could not be legible to the naked eye."[11]

The earliest printed miniature, created in 1468 by the German printer Peter Schoeffer, was the *Diurnale Moguntinum,* a book of days. By the century's end, the popularity of these novel volumes began to swell as printers competed to create the smallest folios. Some of the most wondrous examples were still made by hand, however: in the reign of Elizabeth I, the gentleman calligrapher Peter Bales, famed for his micrographia, produced a handwritten Bible no larger than a hen's egg. "There are as many leaves in his little book as the great Bible, and he hath written as much in one of his little leaves as a great leaf of the Bible," a contemporary observer noted.[12] This tradition was carried well into the twentieth century by practitioners such as W. E. Rudge of Mount Vernon, New York, whose copy of the 1928 New York City phone book measured $4\frac{3}{4}$ by $6\frac{1}{4}$ inches and was $\frac{3}{4}$ inch thick.[13]

The rise of miniature painting, meanwhile, first developed in the form of illuminated manuscripts, holy scriptures embellished with radiantly lucid images. These miniature pictures were cultivated in Islamic and Christian cultures alike. In the West manuscript illuminations grew increasingly elaborate during the Middle Ages, gradually becoming independent of the texts they were meant to illustrate and migrating into the realm of secular art.

It was not until the fifteenth and sixteenth centuries, however, when a vogue for tiny portraits on vellum and ivory swept through Europe, that the miniature proper was born. As defined by the great sixteenth-century English portrait miniaturist, Nicholas Hilliard, painting of this kind should be realized with such diamondlike sharpness that "it seemeth to be the thinge itselfe, even the worke of God and not of man."[14] To achieve this kind of luminous verisimilitude, a limner, as such artists were then known, might spend two years working on a portrait of only a few square inches.

These early miniaturists were concerned less with size than fineness of detail; indeed, the term originally had no connection with the idea of smallness, deriving not from the Latin *minutus*, but from *minium*, the name for the red pigment used in rubricating illuminated manuscripts.[15] With their jewel-like exquisiteness, these portraits were meant to be seen up close, where they could privately and intensively conjure the memory of a loved one.

Over time, the miniature's irresistible charms advanced into coarser arteries of tininess. The seventeenth-century fashion for clockwork toys, the breeding of midget animal species in the eighteenth, and the vogue for model railways in the nineteenth, are all degenerate forms of the miniature proper. Although it developed especially strong roots in the West, this fascination with tiny things transcends cultural boundaries, showing up in such diverse traditions as the Mexican folk art of dressing fleas in elaborate garments and the Japanese custom of breeding dwarfed potted trees, or bonsai, which dates back to the fourteenth century.

Among those who have surveyed this alluring terrain, the French phenomenologist Gaston Bachelard stands as a philosophical giant as well as a most passionate advocate; it is difficult in fact to think of another metaphysician who could match his startling confession, "I feel more at home in miniature worlds." For Bachelard the appeal of diminutive space begins with its capacity for instilling a feeling of omnipotence in the viewer. "The cleverer I am at miniaturising the world," he declared, "the better I possess it."[16]

Endearing and unpretentious, the miniature universe is above all something we look down upon, and Bachelard consequently links it to belfry dreams and the experience of gazing at a distant horizon where the world appears as a minuscule composition. At such moments we feel removed from the ceaseless activity and ungainliness of our immediate surroundings, and we may imbibe a profound tranquility.

Like an opiate, this apparent calm sets us dreaming. In the case of the miniature, we dream of projecting ourselves into its intimate distance—an imaginative leap encouraged by the profound privacy in which every miniature is steeped. Physically we stand outside this Lilliputian domain, and when we imaginatively enter within it, we feel ourselves to be the sole inhabitant. As if paying homage to this principle, the renowned Thorne Rooms of Chicago, a collection of period interiors recreated on a 1:12 scale, typically include evidence of human activity—open books, balls of yarn, teacups—but no human figures, leaving us to imagine ourselves the lone possessor of this theatrical little world.

Miniature thus affords not only a dream of dominance, but a window of escape. Literature presents us with numerous examples of this motif. In a short fragment Hermann Hesse tells of a prisoner who drew a railroad landscape on the wall of his cell and then eluded his jailers by making himself so tiny he could enter his picture, climbing aboard a train just as it disappeared into the darkness of a tunnel. In *The Three Stigmata of Palmer Eldritch*, Philip K. Dick describes a Martian colony whose residents flee their bleak environment by mentally projecting themselves into elaborate Barbie and Ken sets, where they enjoy an idealized earthly existence.[17]

Part of the appeal of miniatures is that they transport us to a world that is more precise and more brilliantly elucidated than our own; shimmering under the halo of the ideal, they provide a charming refuge from the gross physical data and corporeal failings of our ordinary experience. But miniatures evoke far more than a refined version of our everyday reality. Values become strangely enriched at this scale; our entire world outlook is compressed and takes on concentrated power.

Oddly enough, our experience of time in the miniature realm is also concentrated. In an experiment conducted by researchers at the University of Tennessee's School of Architecture, participants were asked to picture themselves in variously scaled miniature lounges and to report whenever they imagined half an hour had passed. The investigators found that as subjects mentally inhabited scale models of decreasing size, their experience of temporal duration was proportionately compressed; that if, for example, "a subject experiences 30 minutes in a 1:12 scale model in 5 minutes of elapsed time, his elapsed time for the same experience in a 1:24 scale model should be 2.5 minutes."[18] Miniature time, in other words, is experienced as if under a magnifying glass, so that a single minute might appear to be ten.

What lures us into this condensed time zone, dimly remembered from childhood, is the density of detail we encounter. Every miniature surface is compacted with a profusion of minutiae, a forest of endless nuance and tiny particulars. And it is precisely this wealth of pullulating and intricate detail that imbues each miniature with the aura of a microcosm, a self-contained universe governed by its own logic and rules. This hothouse atmosphere ensures that no matter how exactly a miniature might reproduce a life-sized object, it inevitably inspires fantasy, comprising an oneiric space where, as we have seen, the viewer is drawn, almost as if by magnetic force, to dreams of domination and escape.[19]

Yet as an object, the reality of the miniature is never in doubt; though reduced in scale, it lies comfortably within the compass of our sensorium. Microminiature art, on the other hand, crosses the borders of our perceptual threshold. Such work cannot be seen with the naked eye, we cannot easily measure its volume and mass, and properly speaking, we can no more touch it than we can a distant star. Its shape and texture remain alien to our fingers.

This simple fact is of great consequence, as it endows the work with an aura of intangibility. A microminiature by Sandaldjian seems to exist not only beyond our reach, but in a reality of its own making. Like a silent interval in the midst of a tumultuous symphony, it occupies a dimension we can neither possess nor dominate.

Nor does it offer a window of escape. Instead, its unfathomable size wreaks havoc on our accustomed notions of physical space and unsettles our faculties of measure. Distance and proximity grow easily confused at this level; when we behold Sandaldjian's art we may feel as though we were looking through the wrong end of a telescope—the work seems far away yet oddly intimate. And in contrast to the miniature's domesticated charm, the microminiature appears sublimely preposterous. It gently mocks us with a mischievous absurdity, as when Sandaldjian shows us *The World* resting on the tip of a needle.

If miniature provokes us to dream, the microminiature is already dreamy itself, possessing an enchanted address. It dwells in a realm of *amusing physics,* a microgravity climate where, as the pioneers of nanotechnology assure us, the normal laws of science do not necessarily hold sway. We are admitted to this territory only through the intervening grace of the microscope, a tool that from its beginnings has been associated with wonder, its great powers of magnification renowned for revealing the secret structure of familiar surfaces and transforming them into a *terra mirabilis.* And we are admitted under very specific conditions: when we examine Sandaldjian's sculpture through its viewing apparatus, we relinquish the world around us and plunge into solitary experience.

This profound privacy, however, has nothing to do with the miniature's nest of reverie-inducing solitude. It is a singular space, but not actually an intimate one: microscopic art is far too tiny to be truly personal or to serve sentimental associations. Haunted by the infinite spaces of the subatomic world, these nearly invisible works conjure a shadowless order of reality. It is for good reason that the microminiaturist usually chooses for his art subjects that eschew individual reference and seem at home on a Platonic plane.

To a large degree, this endows each microminiature with an eerily cerebral quality and the uncanny quiescence of something perceived with the mind's eye—an impression strengthened by the way this work effectively vanishes as soon as we step away from the viewfinder. Observing Sandaldjian's sculpture through the magnifying lens, we do not project ourselves into its space, but on the contrary, it seems to enter our own, as the microscope functions almost like a projector, beaming the image past our retina and onto an interior screen. And the object we perceive there is so astonishingly insubstantial that we may be inclined to wonder where else it might possibly exist but in our mental landscape.

In short, microminiature inhabits a space that relates not to fantasy but metaphysics. This, too, is of tremendous import if we are to glimpse the peculiar nature of our relation with microminiature art and the truths embedded therein.

The great Irish writer Flann O'Brien indirectly explored these matters in *The Third Policeman*, in which he portrayed a microminiaturist of considerable talent. Using a home-made blade whose point is so sharp it cannot be seen, this unusual policeman carves a series of "Chinese boxes," one fitting inside the other, with the smallest diminishing well beyond the borders of the visible.

In similar fashion, every microminiature prompts us to speculate whether there may not be other universes secreted within the world we already know. Are there microsymphonies to which we unwittingly remain deaf? Are microsmells at this very moment wafting undetected past our nostrils? Can there be truth in the musings of mystics who speculate that every atom comprises a universe unto itself, containing a thousand suns?

Certainly biological science suggests that we ourselves are a kind of Chinese box, the whole of our giant life concentrated in a microscopic strand of DNA. Perhaps it is only fitting that more than one microminiaturist has fashioned his work from human hair, a bodily symbol of the crowd and of multitudes beyond number. By such subtle means, an artist like Sandaldjian calls attention to our sublime relationship to the vastness of our body, with its billions of separate cells.

Slowly but surely, then, every microminiature leads us towards the apprehension of this truth: that reality is an endless succession of boxes, levels of perception, theatrical facades, and thus ultimately lies beyond our grasp.

≈≈

All small things, it is said, must evolve slowly, and with patience. The microminiaturist must work with a patience that saturates the artist's every finger, instilling a profound repose in each cell. And it is not only his hands that are involved—the microminiaturist must learn to make his decisive movements between breaths, even between heartbeats, and he must work in monastic solitude, in the nocturnal quiet of a small, clean room.

If we are already impressed by the painstaking craft and endless toil that goes into the creation of miniatures, here we encounter a degree of skill and devotion almost beyond belief. It suggests an almost spiritual discipline; in particular, the self-control required is reminiscent of yogic practices that allow the adept to master his pulse and respiration. For yogis, control of the body provides a pathway for learning to control the mind, and the practice of the microminiaturist likewise embodies a distinct metaphysical aspect.

In the Bible, miracles are frequently enacted to encourage faith, yet in work such as this, it is faith that produces a kind of miracle. Sandaldjian's own credo was a variant of scientific empiricism. His study of ergonomics led him to believe that the most ordinary student, if properly retrained, could become a virtuoso; following the same logic, he believed that anyone who persevered could master the art of microminiatures. And this was a skill, he maintained, that was not limited to art but could have other, as yet unforeseen, applications.

Near the end of his life Sandaldjian hoped to pass his knowledge on to his son, Levon, but he departed this dimension before his wish could be realized. Yet even though the rudiments of microminiature can be taught, just as Kazarian taught them to Sandaldjian, mastery of this art no doubt requires a special calling. The microminiaturist must think like an explorer; he must be willing to probe the limits of space and those of his own unknown talents. And as is true of any endeavor where we aim to go beyond ourselves, aspiration counts for nearly everything.

A tribute to human ingenuity and obsession, Sandaldjian's work stands as a testament to generosity as well.

Without delving into the murky psychological waters of an artist's personal motivation, it seems safe to say that an endeavor like Sandaldjian's must have been fueled in part by a desire to brighten the eyes and hearts of his fellow citizens. His difficult and singular art, practiced by so few in this world, extends to each of us an occasion of irrefutable wonder. There is no more inspiring gift: Francis Bacon considered wonder to be "the seed of knowledge," and to Descartes it was "the first of all the passions."[20]

"An inventive spirit is what separates man from machine," Sandaldjian always insisted. "Man is the real technology." Perhaps this is the final lesson imparted to us by his microminiature sculpture: not only do we produce wonders, but we are wondrous objects in our own right. When we behold Sandaldjian's work and acknowledge the impact of this astounding sensory experience, we also understand that wonder, as much as necessity, is the mother of inquisitiveness and invention. As Vladimir Nabokov remarked, ". . . it is in this childishly speculative state of mind that we know the world to be good."[21]

Sandaldjian would probably have agreed. Each piece of his art remains an abundant reservoir of mystery our questions and researches can never drain. In its presence we may come to know quiet moments of awe that release us from our burdens, which we may then lay down as gently and quietly as dust falls from a bookshelf, dust that this artist of wonder might have fashioned into one more infinitesimal miracle.

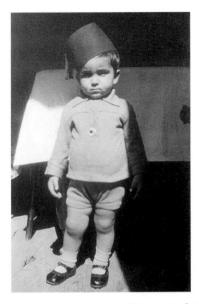

LEFT: *Hagop Sandaldjian in his father's hat at age eighteen months, Cairo.*
RIGHT: *Kindergarten photograph, Haykazian School, Cairo.*

LEFT: *Hagop's father, Khachik Sandaldjian, at age sixty.*
RIGHT: *Hagop's mother, Siranush Sandaldjian,*
at age fifty-six, shortly before her death.

LEFT: *In front of the* Rossia, *which brought the Sandaldjians to Batumi, Armenia, in 1948.*
RIGHT: *With Khachik and Siranush Sandaldjian, at a Black Sea resort, c. 1957.*

At Lake Sevan, 1955.

With Sevan village friends, 1964.

At Lake Sevan, summer 1964.

LEFT: *Hagop Sandaldjian, 1966.*
RIGHT: *With members of the string quartet, at the Yerevan Conservatory.*

LEFT: *In Leninakan, Armenia, at age thirty-one.*
RIGHT: *Grigor Sandaldjian, Hagop's brother, c. 1964.*

*As soloist, performing J. S. Bach's Brandenberg Concerto
with the Armenian Symphony Orchestra, Yerevan, c. 1975.*

*Michael Terian, Hagop Sandaldjian's professor
at the Moscow Conservatory, c. 1973.*

LEFT: *c. 1957.*
RIGHT: *c. 1961.*

At Yerevan studios performing the premiere recording of
Alan Hovannes's Concerto for Violin, 1961.

In the home of Professor Terian, Moscow, 1973.

Yerevan, c. 1977.

Hagop, Levon, Verena, and Siranush, at home in Los Angeles, 1987.

At home in Los Angeles, 1987.

PLATES

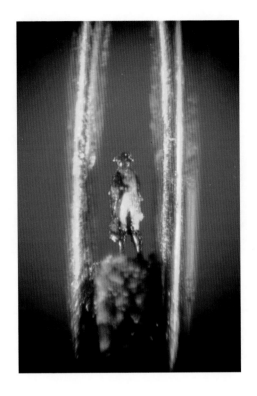

1. NAPOLEON

In the eye of the needle stands the colorful statue of Napoleon on a large pedestal.

2. Aramik

On a strand of hair from the artist's three-month-old grandson stand nine exotic, colorful birds.

3. Broken Dreams

Unfinished portrait. Golden violin with broken neck.
Length is $^1/_{32}$ of an inch.

4. HABANERA

In the eye of the needle is a sculpture of the
Spanish dancer in scarlet dress with her castanets.

———————————

5. AMERICAN INDIAN

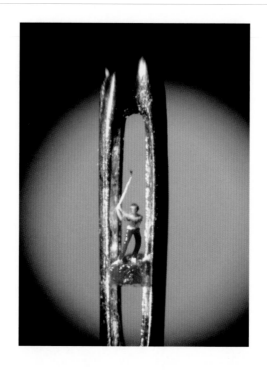

6. THE GOLF PLAYER

*In the eye of the needle, on a green pedestal,
stands the colorful statue of the golf player
keeping high the golf club.*

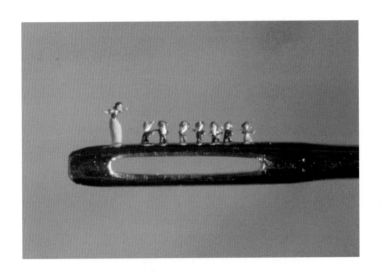

7. SNOW WHITE AND THE SEVEN DWARFS

Five Walt Disney characters installed on needles, plates 7–12.

8. Goofy

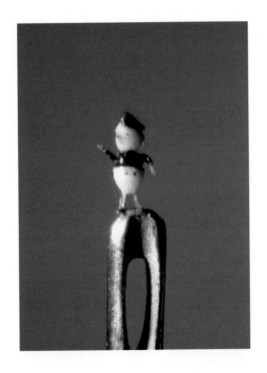

9. PINOCCHIO

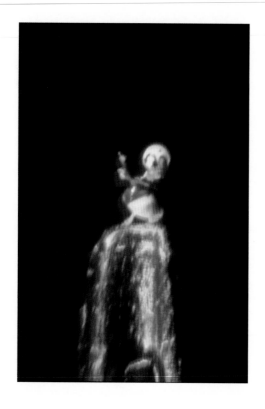

10. DONALD DUCK

11. DONALD DUCK (VERSION TWO)

12. MICKEY MOUSE

13. BASEBALL

The preferred sport of my American friends.
The sculpture of the baseball player is installed
on the edge of the needle.

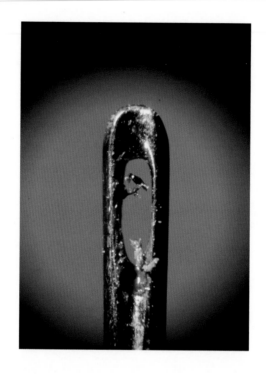

14. THE FOX AND THE CROW, LA FONTAINE

*In the eye of the needle the crow is seated
on the branch of a tree, keeping a piece of
cheese in his beak, while the cunning fox is
asking the crow to sing a song.*

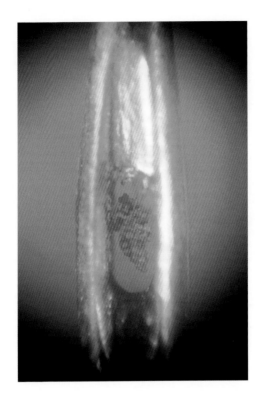

15. PROSPERITY

*A cluster of red grapes is suspended
in the eye of a sewing-machine needle.*

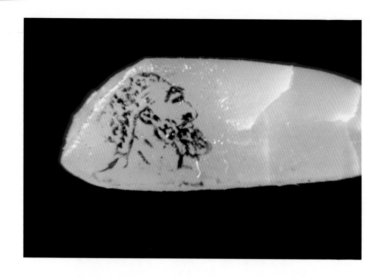

16. Mesrob Mashtotz

On a grain of rice is the portrait of the creator of the Armenian alphabet: an expression of love and respect.

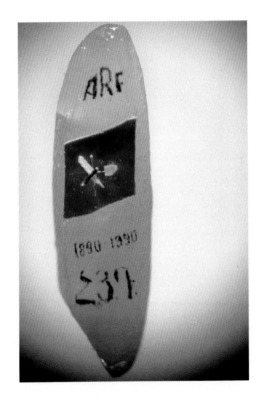

17. ARF

*Grain of rice created in commemoration of the
hundredth-year anniversary of the Armenian Revolutionary Federation.*

18. THE BIRD

*The symbol of peace is made on the
sharp tip of a needle.*

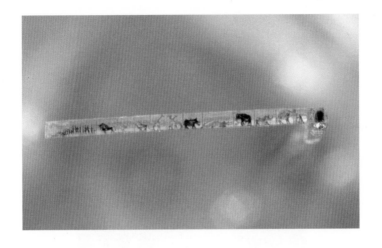

19. WILD ANIMALS

*On a strand of hair twelve wild animals are seen in the
presence of a crowd. The strand of hair is covered with glue.*

20. Dancer on a Fig Seed

21. Cio-Cio San

The figure of a woman sculpted on a strand of the artist's white hair.
An expression of admiration for the opera of Puccini's Madame Butterfly.

22. Crucifix

The cross consists of a bisection of a
single strand of human hair. The statue of
the crucified Christ is made of gold.

23. Eternal Symbol (Mount Ararat)

*On a grain of rice, my beloved mountain. From the times
of Noah up to this day, "you stand supreme and majestic."*

24. Autosculpture

In the eye of the needle stretches the artist's black hair,
on which stands the autosculpture of his own head.

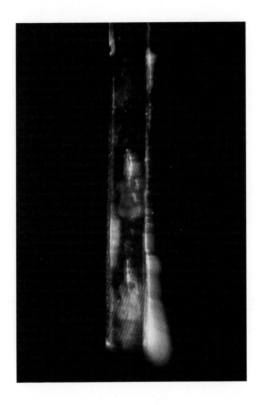

25. SAFETY PLACE

*A Viole d'Amour and Citar violin inserted
in a strand of hair of the artist.*

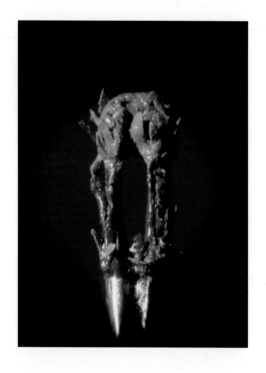

26. LITTLE RED RIDING HOOD

*On the bottom of the needle eye, between huge trees,
one can see Little Red Riding Hood.*

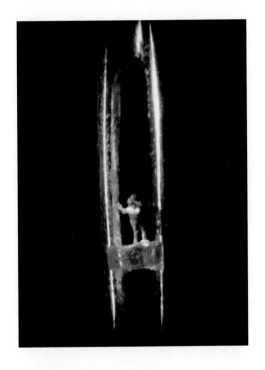

27. THE KID

*Who can predict what the sloppy and energetic kid
will become when he grows up?*

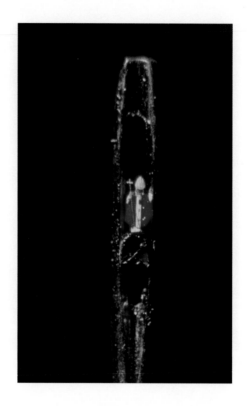

28. Pope John

*In the eye of the needle, on a large
pedestal, stands the statue of John Paul II
in full, colorful papal regalia.*

29. MAY ALL YOUR DREAMS COME TRUE

*Best wishes from the artist to each and all who appreciate
this work of art. It's inscribed on a strand of hair of the artist.*

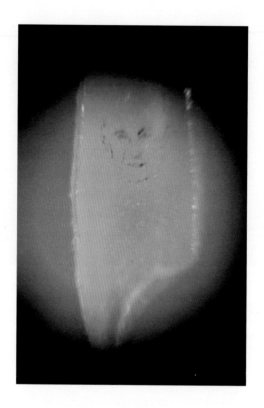

30. ETUDE I

Unfinished portrait.

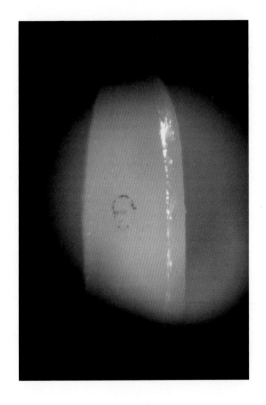

31. ETUDE 2

Unfinished portrait.

NOTES

1. In terms of a handmade object of comparable size to Sandaldjian's work, one thinks of William McClelland's parts kit for a motor no bigger than $1/64$th of a cubic inch. Forged with sharpened toothpicks, a watchmaker's lathe, and a microdrill press, it was made in the early 1960s in response to a challenge issued by physicist Richard Feynman during his 1959 lecture "There's Plenty of Room at the Bottom." McClelland's parts kit was included in the The Museum of Jurassic Technology's 1993 exhibition *Nanotechnology: Machines in the Microscopic Realm*.

Long before the advent of micromachines, silicon chips, and transistors, however, modernization had already been equated with shrinking dimensions. Gail Borden, the nineteenth-century condensed-milk magnate, typified this outlook with his conviction that the industrial age did not permit things "to stretch out in time and space as they once had. A declaration of love was distilled to a kiss, a sermon to an aphorism. . . . 'I mean to put a potato into a pillbox, a pumpkin into a tablespoon,' he declared." See Thomas Hine, *The Total Package: The Evolution of Boxes,*

Bottles, Cans, Tubes, and Other Persuasive Containers (Boston: Little, Brown, 1995), 69.

Given the venerable history of the association between diminishing scale and modernity, the claim that microminiature is the art of the future does not seem entirely without merit.

2. All quotes from Sandaldjian originally appeared in Serge L. Samoniantz, "The Miniature World of H. Sandaldjian," *The Asbare͂ English Edition*, May 16, 1987, p.20.

The estimate that there are only four or five living microminiaturists in the world is one that appears frequently in the limited literature on this subject, but to this author's knowledge, no accurate census has yet been undertaken.

3. Sandaldjian's ergonomic method also involved specific exercises designed to enhance the fingers' suppleness and tactile sensitivity, which are essential for control and mastery of an instrument.

4. Hagop Sandaldjian, "The Significance of Ergonomics in the Methods of Violin and Viola Performance," unpublished manuscript, c. 1988.

5. *A Treatise Concerning the Arte of Limning*, annual published by the Walpole Society, vol. 1, Oxford, 1912. Certain contemporary microminiaturists take equally extreme precautions; Nikolai Syadristy of Kiev, for example, wets down his entire body before beginning work and wears only his undershorts as he works.

6. Howard Witt, "Art's Minute Man: Ukrainian Microminiature Sculptor Stands Tall," *Chicago Tribune*, August 1, 1993.

7. For more on the link between Leibniz and microminiature, see Vitaly Chermayev, "Invisible Legacy: The Philosophy of Leibniz Considered in Its Aesthetic Consequences" (doctorate thesis, University of Manchester, 1989).

8. J. L. Propert, *A History of Miniature Art with Notes on Collectors and Collections* (London: Macmillan and Co., 1887), 178.

9. Gaston Paris, *Le Petit Poucet et la Grande Ourse* (Paris: 1875), in Gaston Bachelard, *The Poetics of Space,* trans. Maria Jolas (Boston: Beacon Press, 1994).

10. Witt, op cit.

11. Isaac D'Israeli, *Curiosities of Literature,* vol. 1 (London: Dover, 1924), 275.

12. Ibid., 275.

13. See Susan Stewart, *On Longing: Narratives of the Miniature, the Gigantic, the Souvenir, the Collection* (Durham, North Carolina: Duke University Press, 1993), 42. It should be noted that Rudge wrote out his copy of the phone book by hand. The smallest printed book with cursive material to be published in modern times is an edition of "Old King Cole!" which measured 1 mm x 1 mm and was published in March 1985 by The Glennifer Press, Paisley, Scotland. Printed on 22-gsm paper, its pages are so thin that they can be turned only with the use of a needle.

Micrographists typically applied their talents to texts that described an entire world, sublime tomes suggestive of a genius beyond human origin (e.g., the Bible and the New York phone book). In miniaturizing such a work, one is drawn closer not to its contents, but its mystery, which is reduced to a form that is at once charming and domesticated, the way an evil spirit or genie may be safely contained within a small bottle. Shrunk to the size of jewelry, a book can play an intimate role in our daily life; miniature Bibles were often fastened to a chain and worn around the neck.

In our own age, nanotechnologists have reproduced texts that can only be discerned with an electron microscope. Using electron-beam lithography in 1985, a team of electrical engineering graduate students at Stanford University copied the opening page of *A Tale of Two Cities* onto the head of a pin, at a 1/25,000 scale reproduction. For more on this *ne plus ultra* of micrographia, see Ed Regis, *Nano: The Emerging Science of Nano-technology: Remaking the World—Molecule by Molecule* (Boston: Little, Brown, 1985). (I am indebted to Lawrence Weschler for bringing this work to my attention.)

14. Raymond Lister, *The Miniature Defined* (Cambridge: The Golden Head Press, 1963), 2.

15. Ibid., 5. Lister goes on to mention that the use of the term *miniature* to denote other small objects—a miniature book, a minia-ture dog—is a corruption introduced in the eighteenth century.

16. Bachelard, op cit., 150.

17. Ibid. The fragment by Hesse originally appeared in the Algerian-based French literary review *Fontaine*, no. 57, p. 725, pub-lished during the Second World War. Philip K. Dick, *The Three Stigmata of Palmer Eldritch* (New York: Vintage Books, 1991).

It is curious that in prompting dreams of both dominance and escape, the miniature seems to cater, however delicately, to our dual legacy as an animal that hunted and was in turn preyed upon by other species.

18. Alton J. Delong, "Phenomenological Space-Time: Toward an Experiential Relativity," *Science*, August 7, 1981, pp. 681–82. In the experiment participants were shown variously scaled miniature lounges with scale figures. They were asked to imagine themselves as the scale figure, to identify appropriate lounge activities, and then to "inform the investigator when they subjectively felt (not thought) the scale figure had been engaged in the activity in the scale model environment for 30 minutes." (This remarkable experi-ment first came to my attention in Susan Stewart's *On Longing*).

19. An historical example of this oneiric power is provided by the origin of Disneyland, which was dreamed up by Walt Disney while he was riding the miniature train that snaked through his backyard. One might also consider the profusion of whimsical

motifs and topographies that distinguish miniature golf from its full-scale counterpart: the dizzying collage of castles, windmills, lighthouses, jungle lagoons, steepled churches, igloos, dinosaurs, etc. When we shrink our world, it seems that no reality is ever so distant as to be beyond our grasp, and we inevitably drift towards reverie.

20. John Onians, " 'I wonder . . .' : A Short History of Amazement," in *Bearers of Meaning: The Classical Orders in Antiquity, the Middle Ages and the Renaissance* (Princeton: Princeton University Press, 1990), 18.

21. Vladimir Nabokov, *Lectures on Literature*, ed. Fredson Bowers (New York: Harcourt Brace Jovanovich, 1980), 374.

c. 1975

A Look into the Ergonomics Method of Violin Teaching

Under the Light of Ergonomics Science

Ergonomics is an applied science, which is based on an individual's physiology, anatomy, psychology, hygiene, and other sciences as well.

The purpose is to simplify the task or work process and to implement maximum success and results. Under this applied science it became possible to enlighten the conflicting viewpoints of the violin methodologists, bring their viewpoints into clearer understanding, and touch upon agile and dexterous ways of playing.

This particular method has been accepted by the highest noted authorities at the Moscow Supreme Certifying Commission and is implemented at the Moscow Chaikovsky Conservatory and at the Armenian Academy of Arts Institute (USSR).

The discussion of Ergonomics in relation to the violin is based upon the founder of this field, Professor Hagop Sandaldjian.

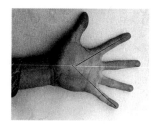

In nature every process independent of human cognition has its prime and best theory. Theories of various processes so far known to mankind are different by their essence. The theory of a technical process must foresee every single possibility which may take place in that process. The theory of violin performance has a different stand.

The objectives of violin techniques, appearing after the era of empiricism and up-to-date, had been based on the apprehension and generalization of the development process of violin performance. It is obvious that the basis of evolutional development of violin performance had not been its theory. It is true that the art of musical performance, as a certain type of work fulfilled by man, differs from other labor processes by the specific creative nature of its objective. The specifics are reflected in the creative substantiation of the musical mind, when under the magic of the art and when the musical features expressed by the performer are perceived by the audience. However, the theory of any process is based on its means. The means of the process of violin performance are the possibilities of the violin player. These are the possibilities of brain, a person's spiritual properties, and anatomophysiological capabilities. In today's violin theories we see neither a thorough application nor a practical use of the achievements of the above-mentioned sciences which are so essential for the theory violin performance.

It is believed that the introduction of scientific, Ergonomical achievements will help a great deal in the progress of violin theory and will complement the existing methods which are the accomplishments of famous violinists and pedagogues. However, in these methods one can feel the subjective approach of the authors.

An example of a conflicting viewpoint: L. Auer, C. Flesh, Uberhart, and others complained about the weakness and ineffectiveness of the little finger and therefore suggested daily exercises to strengthen this particular finger. On the other hand, I. Voicu and others following his school of thought felt that the weakness of the pinky is not irrelevant, therefore, I. Voicu ignored the exercises suggested by their opponents.

We should note that I. Voicu was responsible for teaching and producing many exceptional violinists too. Naturally, these great masters were unfamiliar with the science of Ergonomical characterization of motion necessary for musical performance-characterization which would make the theory of violin of prime importance. So far in the existing techniques of violin performance the external aspect of the process is explained, while for the characterization of the theory of a physiological process the external aspect alone cannot be satisfying.

In the first place, the theory of violin techniques must ensure the Ergonomical shaping of necessary movements which shall be based on a prime and objective theory. The question is: for the above process which are the Ergonomical modes of motion and what are the means of achieving them?

Ergonomics states that "the full value of motional effect depends on functional conditions, on forces which are produced within inner and outer body conditions. The nonconformity in the use of these

forces through position and their relation to position is reflected in fullworthiness of motion."

During the process of performance the inner force is produced through contraction of muscles. The outer force is the terrestrial gravitational force. The various interrelation of muscular and gravitational forces is the source of different modes of motion. According to Ergonomics, every mode of motion demands its own hand position.

Consequently, the more gravity is used in this process the hand positioning is less muscle contraction oriented and vice versa (more muscle contraction = less gravity). Each variation requires its appropriate hand position. This rule applies for both hands.

Thus, when the inner strength of contraction in finger muscles is dominated then the weakness of the pinky is emphasized and obvious, because contraction and relaxing muscles of the pinky are weak. Where the dominating

strength is the gravity the pinky has enough power to weigh down. In this, exercises that have been created to strengthen the pinky are no longer as useful as they could be.

As we see, the reasons for these conflicting viewpoints are: being satisfied only by the use of one of the three factors: the anatomic factor. Whereas the Ergonomics method of research is based on the relationship of those three factors: anatomic, physiological, and psychological. To date, the neglect of the role of mode of motion has had a negative effect on the process of violin instruction. In many cases even talented students have never been able to express their inner world and all instruction efforts have been almost wasted.

For the technique of performance, it's necessary to set performing capabilities and formation of conditional reflexes only through which music is produced; at that point, the violinist is so well versed with the latter that he does not have to think about means of performance because, thanks to

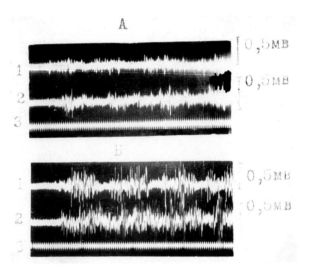

reflexes, all the necessary means are subjected to his will at first demand. In our method, the formation process of motion reflexes depend on:

(1) artistic audition
(2) activation of feedback between center and periphery
(3) activation functions of the neural system necessary for performance
(4) gradual hardening of the method of instruction and objective way of training.

The objective way of training in its turn depends on the mean volume of motion, smoothness, energy saving, and condition prompted by physiology of labor which ensure the usefulness of motion.

During numerous pedagogical experiments, it was clarified that through the rational use of gravitational forces and proper position, the intuition of the performer, thanks to his purposefulness, is getting activated to such an extent that the conditionalities of the science of labor physiology are taking place mainly by intuition.

The practical significance of our method is imparted through the psychological exercises presented therein, which are activating the necessary functions of the neural system, synthesizing in a practical manner the assigned subject, and ensuring the use of gravitational mode and corresponding position.

The suppleness achieved through the exercises allows the violinist to take the utmost advantage of his fingers' tac-

Teaching a young student, Yerevan, 1966.

Hagop Sandaldjian with students at the
Komitas Music School, Los Angeles, c. 1985.

tile corpuscles and enables him to substantiate every conceived musical nuance.

In our method the position of the left hand is discussed in detail. The text of the exercises deals with the three-octave scales. The objective is the pre-hearing of beautiful sounding during systematized rests and foreseeing of condition assuring the quality of motion. Shortly, through repetitions, these are converted to conditional reflexes and skills. The achievement of pre-hearing capability helps the fore-hearing of the musical mind which is the primary condition for performative and artistical creative thinking. Let us not forget that the repetitions of motion do not guarantee its corrective propriety. Unfavorable motions are also converted to conditional reflexes, hampering progress. The primary role of the instructor is to fight against these hampering reflexes.

The Ergonomics method of violin teaching makes the teaching process more productive, it simplifies the task or work process to implement maximum success and results. It also saves the time and energy of the student and the teacher as well.

This method can be applied theoretically as well as practically to other instruments.

The Museum would like to thank Thomas Barron, Jim Fox, Joshua Kircher, Laura Lindgren, Rex Ravenelle, Ralph Rugoff, Sarah Simons, and Ken Swezey for their kind and generous efforts in the production of this book. We would also like to thank Judith and Stuart Spence, who created the original ties between the Museum and Hagop Sandaldjian. And finally, we would especially like to thank the Sandaldjian family, whose boundless generosity and enduring patience provided the nurturing soil from which these pages were able to grow.

Society for the Diffusion of Useful Information Press
9091 Divide Place, West Covina, California 0x2 6DP

Billings Bogata Bhopa Beirut
Bowling Green Buenos Aires Campton
Dayton Dar es Salaam Düsseldorf
Fort Wayne Indianapolis Lincoln
Mal en Beg Mal en Mor
Nannin Pretoria Teheran
Socorro Terra Haute Ulster

Published in the United States by
The Society for the Diffusion of Useful Information
© 1996 The Museum of Jurassic Technology
9341 Venice Boulevard, Los Angeles, California 90034
Published in cooperation with the Visitors to the Museum
by the Delegates of the Press

ISBN 0-9647215-1-1

Designed by Laura Lindgren
The text of this book was set in Fournier.

Printed in Hong Kong by Oceanic Graphic Printing

10 9 8 7 6 5 4 3 2 1